D1162798

Making a New Nation

EXPLORING THE AMERICAS

Ted Schaefer

HEINEMANN LIBRARY
CHICAGO, ILLINOIS

© 2007 Heinemann Library
a division of Reed Elsevier Inc.
Chicago, Illinois

Customer Service   888–454–2279

Visit our website at www.heinemannraintree.com

Designed by Philippa Baile and Kim Miracle
Maps by Jeff Edwards
Printed and bound in China by WKT Company Limited

11 10 09 08 07
10 9 8 7 6 5 4 3 2 1

Library of Congress Cataloging-in-Publication Data
Schaefer, Ted, 1948-
  Exploring the Americas / Ted Schaefer.
    p. cm. -- (Making a new nation)
  Includes bibliographical references and index.
  ISBN 1-4034-7826-0 (library binding-hardcover) -- ISBN 1-4034-7833-3 (pbk.)
  1. America--Discovery and exploration--European--Juvenile literature.
  2. America--History--To 1810--Juvenile literature. I. Title. II. Series.
  E121.S37 2006
  970.01--dc22
                                    2006003246

Acknowledgments
The author and publisher are grateful to the following for permission to reproduce
copyright material: Alamy Images/Classic Image p. **21**; Alamy Images/North Wind
Picture Archives pp. **9**, **19**, **39**; Corbis pp. **23** (Gianni Dagli Orti), **33** (Joel W. Roger),
36 (Nathan Benn), **37** (Richard A. Cooke), **32**, **35**; Corbis/Bettmann pp. **14**, **20**, **24**;
Corbis/Free Agents Limited p. **8**; Corbis/Historical Picture Archive p. **22**; Corbis Sygma/
Lorpresse p. **25** (J. C. Kanny); Getty Images/AFP p. **17** (Vanderlei Almeida); Getty
Images p. **40** (Alex Wong); Getty Images/Archive Photos p. **29**; Getty Images/Hulton
Archive pp. **6**, **18**; Getty Images/MPI p. **10**; Getty Images/National Geographic p. **34**;
Getty Images/Stock Montage p. **41**; Getty Images/Stone p. **43**; Getty Images/Taxi
p. **5**; Getty Images/Time Life Pictures p. **4**; Harcourt Education Ltd p. **31** (Tristan
Boyer); Mary Evans Picture Library pp. **13**, **30**; Robert Harding p. **28** (Hans Peter
Merten); Topfoto/Fotomas pp. **7**, **27**, **38**.

Cover photograph reproduced with the permission of North Wind/North Wind
Picture Archives.

The publishers would like to thank Brad Martin for his assistance in the preparation of
this book.

Every effort has been made to contact copyright holders of any material reproduced in
this book. Any omissions will be rectified in subsequent printings if notice is given to
the publisher.

CONTENTS

Some words are shown in bold, **like this**. You can find out what they mean by looking in the glossary.

EXPLORING AND DISCOVERING

Long ago, people gathered food such as berries and nuts. They knew the best places to catch fish or hunt rabbits. If the berries were all gone and the fish were not biting, it was time to search somewhere else. They would explore new lands until they found a new home.

After thousands of years, people learned to grow crops and raise animals for food. Groups of people lived together and helped each other. If everyone had enough food, people did not have the same need to explore—but many still did.

In the late 1400s and 1500s, a wave of **explorers** came from Europe to the Americas. They were not looking for food and water. They hoped to find trade routes and rich new lands.

Early people were the first explorers, searching for food and water.

A HAZARDOUS LIFE

Exploring has always been a dangerous pursuit. It can include hazards such as bad weather, accidents like falling or drowning, sickness or disease, and the threat of wild animals. Explorers also run the risk of becoming lost or meeting unfriendly people.

Many explorers went out and never returned. Many of their names have been forgotten. A **discoverer**, on the other hand, is usually remembered. A discoverer is someone who found something and lived to return and tell about it. They are celebrated because they made discoveries that changed the world.

Exploring is still dangerous today. Most discoveries on Earth have been made, so now explorers look toward the stars.

TWO WORLDS

The explorers described in this book came from countries in Europe, sometimes called the Old World. These explorers discovered people, land, and animals that they had never seen before. This "New World" would later be known as the Americas.

For thousands of years, these two worlds grew and developed separately from each other. By 1400 there were millions of people living in Europe and in the Americas. These **continents** had many things in common. Both had large areas of land with many cities and villages where people lived as farmers, artists, and craftspeople. People on both continents developed new farming techniques. There were social structures and governments in both worlds. Sometimes they traded, and sometimes they fought. These two worlds were similar in many ways, but neither knew of the other.

In Europe, new inventions made it possible for explorers to travel farther than ever before, and they did. Soon the two worlds would meet.

By 1500 Lisbon, Portugal, in Europe, was an important shipping port.

RICH NEW WORLD

Thousands of years earlier, when the first people arrived in North America, they traveled over a land bridge (see below). Food was easy to find and the population grew. Over thousands of years, people moved and **settled** throughout the Americas.

When the ice age ended, the glaciers melted and the oceans covered the land bridge. Water surrounded the Americas. The people who had **migrated** were now cut off from the other continents. They lived undisturbed in their own world for more than 10,000 years.

The Aztec city Tenochtitlán, in Mexico, existed long before European explorers arrived in the Americas.

The land bridge

People first lived in Europe, Asia, and Africa more than 40,000 years ago. At that time in the Americas, there were many kinds of animals, but no people. Then, about 20,000 years ago, an ice age froze much of Earth's water into glaciers. The oceans receded and new land was uncovered. A land bridge was formed between Asia and North America. This is how people first came to the Americas.

CHANGING PEOPLES

People gradually changed as they migrated across the Americas. These new continents were so large that groups of people often did not have any neighbors. When they moved into a new area with a different **climate** or food supply, they learned new ways of living. Some groups even developed their own languages.

Most Native Americans formed **tribes** or small communities. Larger groups who spoke the same language are often called peoples. A people might consist of a few tribes living in small villages. The largest groups, like the Aztecs, had a population of millions living over a wide area.

In some ways, the lives of the Native Americans seemed simple. They made tools from wood, bone, and stone. They lived in small homes close to the land. All but the most important people wore simple clothing. However, most Native American **civilizations** were highly developed. They had skilled farmers, complex systems of religion, and a deep artistic tradition.

Some early Native American peoples built beautiful cities.

EUROPEAN CULTURE

European **culture** varied from country to country. But in most places, the culture was at least partly shaped by trade and competition. Countries in Europe traded goods and ideas with each other and with countries in Africa and Asia.

By 1400 Europeans had learned a lot about the world. Their maps showed Europe, Africa, and parts of Asia. They were familiar with the Mediterranean Sea and the Atlantic Ocean, which they called the Ocean Sea. But no European knew what was across the Atlantic. Mapmakers labeled the edges of maps with "unknown."

The printing press

Before the 1400s, books had to be copied by hand. This made them expensive and rare. The invention of the printing press in the 1450s made books cheaper and widely available. Explorers, writers, and scientists could share their information with anyone who could read. By the year 1500, more than 200 European cities had print shops.

The First Printing Press.

After the invention of the printing press, even ordinary people could own books.

RELIGION IN EUROPE

The **era** of exploration was a time of great change in Europe. One of the biggest changes had to do with religion. Before the 1500s, all the Christians in Europe followed more or less the same religion. However, some Christians began to be unhappy with the way the church was run. They eventually split away from the old church. This new faith was called Protestantism.

EUROPEAN EXPLORERS

No matter if they were Catholic or Protestant, Europeans were still Christian. They believed that Christianity was the only true religion and that God was on their side. They felt superior to the other civilizations they met in Africa and Asia. Many thought that serving God meant **converting** others to Christianity or killing those who would not change.

Catholic countries, such as Spain, were often at war with Protestant countries, such as England. Exploration was connected to these wars. Each side was eager to find new lands and to convert more people to its own religion.

*Exploring parties usually included a priest or **missionary**.*

These European countries grew from their exchange of ideas, information, and goods.

A RACE FOR RICHES

The other major motivation for explorers, and for the countries that sent them, was money. Traveling and trading were important parts of life in Europe. Spain alone had hundreds of merchant ships that traveled around the Mediterranean and down the west coast of Africa, hauling trade goods.

Explorers really wanted to go the "Indies." This is what they called a large area of Asia that included China, Japan, and India. Desirable products, such as silk cloth, spices, and pearls, were found in the Indies, but there were no easy **routes** there from Europe. A better trade route would be worth a fortune.

Explorers set out to find new routes and opportunities. A good explorer had to be brave and ambitious. Some were cruel and ruthless as well. The Spanish had a special word for them: **conquistadors**.

DISCOVERING THE AMERICAS

None of the European explorers were actually looking for the Americas. They did not even know they were there. Instead, they wanted to find new ways to reach the Indies. Some crossed the Atlantic toward the south and west. Others sailed to the northwest. Whichever way they went, the explorers kept running into the New World.

To the Native Americans, it was not a New World at all. It was their world and their home. These people had lived in the Americas for at least 20,000 years.

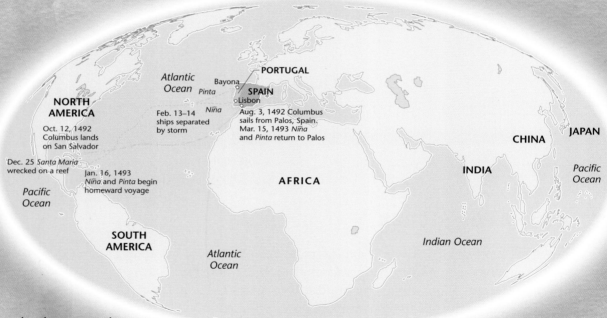

Columbus wanted to sail to the Indies. Instead, he reached the New World.

Native Americans

The word *native* can be confusing because it has two meanings. A person born in a country is considered to be a native of that country. But *native* can also mean to have an origin or beginning in a country, meaning a person's **ancestors** have always lived there. Under this definition, the peoples living in the Americas were not native because their ancestors had come from Asia. But we call them Native Americans because they were the first people to live in the Americas.

COLUMBUS'S FIRST VOYAGE

Christopher Columbus was an experienced sailor. His whole life was spent learning how to sail ships across open seas. He studied maps and books and talked with other explorers. He became convinced that a ship could reach the Indies by sailing west from Spain.

Columbus wanted to prove his theory, but **expeditions** were expensive. He needed a **sponsor**. Columbus finally convinced King Ferdinand and Queen Isabella of Spain to give him three ships with supplies for a long **voyage**. These ships, named the *Niña*, the *Pinta*, and the *Santa Maria*, set sail from Spain on August 3, 1492.

This expedition was a very bold adventure. Columbus and his crews would sail for days over the empty ocean. The crews became fearful after being out of sight of land for so long. Columbus constantly talked to his crews, reminding them of the wealth and glory they would share after a successful journey.

The three ships that Columbus sailed to the New World were tiny and made of wood.

A DIFFICULT JOURNEY

As the ships sailed on, Columbus was worried, too, but he could not let the crew members know. They were already angry and afraid. Finally, after 37 days at sea, they spotted an island and landed on the shore. Columbus planted a flag and claimed the island for Spain.

Native Americans called Taínos lived on the island. They were farmers and fishermen who lived a simple life. The Taínos were friendly toward Columbus and exchanged small gifts with him.

Columbus named the island where he first landed San Salvador.

Columbus's log
These words come from the log, or diary, that Columbus kept on his first voyage:
September 24, 1492
I am having serious trouble with the crew ... All day long and all night long those who are awake and able to get together never cease to talk to each other in circles, complaining that they will never be able to return home. I am told by a few trusted men that if I persist in going onward, the best course of action will be to throw me into the sea some night.

ISLANDS AND INDIANS

Columbus and his crews sailed to other islands in the Caribbean, including Cuba and Hispaniola, and claimed them also. He thought all the islands were part of the Indies, so he called the native people Indians.

COLUMBUS SAILS AGAIN

When Columbus and his men returned to Spain, they were greeted as heroes. They had crossed an uncharted ocean and claimed new lands. But they did not bring back gold or find a new trade route, as the queen had hoped. Several months later, Columbus sailed again. He guided seventeen ships west to Hispaniola. Columbus explored dozens of islands, searching for gold. None was found because these islands had very little gold.

Columbus made several additional trips to the New World, still searching for a route to the Indies. He died without realizing that the lands he found were just as rich.

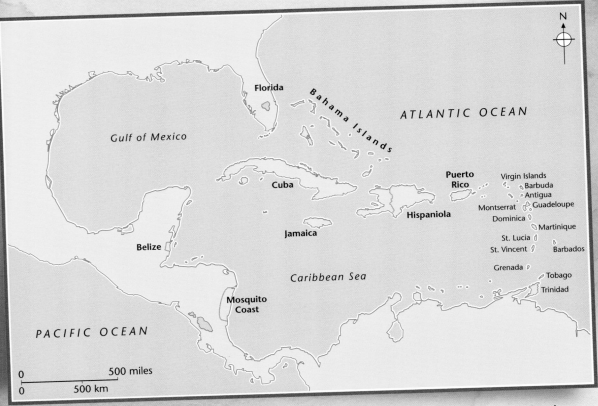

The first European explorers to reach the Americas landed on these Caribbean islands.

ENGLAND'S FIRST CLAIM IN THE AMERICAS

After Columbus returned successfully, others were eager to follow his lead. John Cabot was one of them. King Henry VII of England wanted to find new trade routes. He gave Cabot a small ship and crew. They sailed from England in 1497.

A month later, John Cabot and his men sighted the coast of North America. He landed and claimed it for England. After exploring for a month, Cabot sailed back and reported to the king.

King Henry was pleased with Cabot's report and gave him more ships to make another voyage. In 1498 Cabot sailed west with five ships. One was damaged and sailed back. The others were never heard from again.

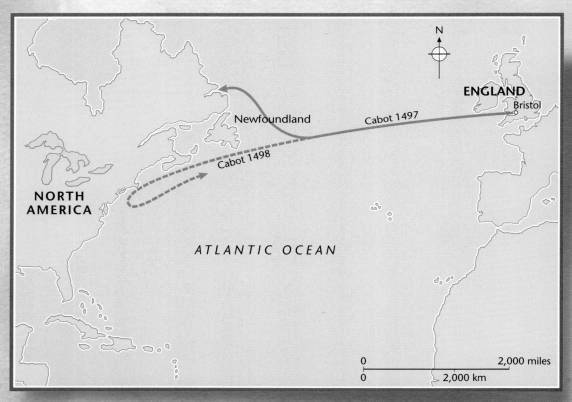

John Cabot was the first man to claim a part of North America for England.

The Northwest Passage

Once Europeans realized that North America was an entire continent, it was at first considered a problem. They wanted to find a way around it to reach Asia. Explorers sailed north and west, up rivers and into bays, seeking a northwest **passage** through North America. Although they searched for many years, no usable passage was ever found.

FIRST EUROPEAN IN SOUTH AMERICA

Pedro Álvares Cabral was a Portuguese explorer. King Manuel of Portugal sent Cabral on an expedition with thirteen ships. This fleet set out on March 8, 1500, with plans to sail around the southern tip of Africa to reach the Indian Ocean and trade goods with the people there.

The ships sailed far out into the Atlantic Ocean to avoid the rough seas near the coast. They sailed farther and farther until a tall mountain was spotted in the distance.

At first they thought it was an island, but a closer look showed the long coastline of a huge land. Cabral went ashore, set up a giant wooden cross, and claimed the land for Portugal. This land was later **colonized** by Portugal and is now called Brazil. People there speak Portuguese and celebrate Cabral as the founder of their country.

In Brazil today, people still speak Portuguese.

AMERIGO VESPUCCI

Amerigo Vespucci was born in Florence, Italy, in 1454. He was educated by priests and went to work in Spain, where he helped manage a company that outfitted ships to make long voyages.

In 1499 Vespucci convinced Spanish rulers to pay for a voyage of exploration. He sailed from Spain with four ships full of crew and supplies. They crossed the Atlantic Ocean and reached the coast of South America. After traveling south along the coast, the expedition turned around and sailed north.

In 1501 Vespucci made another voyage, this time in the service of Portugal. Once again he reached South America and traveled far south down the coast. He was surprised to realize how big the Americas were. He sent letters back to Europe to tell of his discoveries.

The Americas were named to honor the explorer Amerigo Vespucci.

AMERICUS VESPUTIUS

OF THE CARAVEL SANTA MARIA, COLUMBUS'S SHIP, ON THE COAST OF HISPANIOLA, DEC. 24, 1492.

Stormy seas were dangerous to small ships.

WHO DISCOVERED THE AMERICAS?

Columbus did not discover the Americas. Native Americans were the first people there. Columbus was not even the first European to reach the Americas. **Vikings** had sailed from northern Europe to North America 500 years earlier. But the Vikings did not make permanent **settlements** there.

WHO NAMED THE AMERICAS?

These new continents were named after Amerigo Vespucci, even though he did not discover them. Vespucci wrote about his voyages and was the first person to call the discoveries a "New World." A mapmaker put "Amerigo's Land" on a map of the newly found continents and from then on, they have been called America, or the Americas.

The life of an explorer

Daily life for early explorers was difficult and dangerous. On their ships, fresh water was limited, and food was often spoiled and full of worms. The explorers were exposed to harsh weather, diseases, and unfriendly Native Americans. Many expeditions were wiped out by sickness and accidents. Even so, there were always people willing to go on expeditions. If they were successful, the explorers could become very rich.

EXPLORING THE CARIBBEAN

Once Columbus had shown the way, everyone knew how to reach the New World. The exploration rush was on. Explorers set out in ships to see what they could find and to take what they could keep. Many sailed first to Hispaniola.

Hispaniola soon became a Spanish base. From there, explorers sailed in all directions. Many other islands in the Caribbean Sea were discovered and claimed. Some explorers traveled southwest across the Caribbean Sea to South America. Other expeditions sailed west into the Gulf of Mexico and on to present-day Panama and Mexico.

Ponce de Leon was governor of Puerto Rico for three years, until he decided to become an explorer again.

Ponce de Leon

Some men who were members of early expeditions later became leaders. Juan Ponce de León arrived in Hispaniola with Columbus in 1493, but a few years later King Ferdinand of Spain sent him to conquer Puerto Rico. After Ponce de Leon took Puerto Rico, he established a **colony** there in 1509 and ruled as governor.

THE DISCOVERY OF THE PACIFIC OCEAN

Vasco Núñez de Balboa was an explorer whose ship had crashed on rocks near Hispaniola. He had been there for several years. He owed people money, and no one who was in debt was allowed to leave Hispaniola. Balboa heard of an expedition that was leaving the island. He hid in a barrel on one of the ships just before it sailed. Later, he became part of the crew.

The men sailed west until they reached the land that is now Panama. They founded a settlement at Darién. Balboa was popular, and so King Ferdinand appointed him **governor**. Unlike most other governors, Balboa tried to get along with the Native Americans living in the area and treated them fairly.

The Native Americans told stories about a great sea to the west. Balboa led 180 Spanish soldiers and 800 Native Americans on a difficult journey over mountains and through swamps. In 1513 he became the first European to see the Pacific Ocean from the Americas.

Balboa claimed the Pacific Ocean and all the lands touching it for Spain.

CONQUISTADORS

Hernando Cortés was born in Spain in 1485. His parents sent him to the University of Salamanca to become a lawyer. Cortés was a good student, but he left school after two years. He had heard stories of adventure and wanted to be an explorer.

Cortés's life as an adventurer started out slowly. He traveled to Hispaniola in 1504. For seven years, he ran a farm where Native Americans worked as **slaves**. Then, Cortés joined an expedition that colonized Cuba. He grew rich, but he still wanted more.

The Spanish heard stories of people living in lands to the west who had vast amounts of gold. In 1519 Cortés sailed west to find them. He had eleven ships and about 600 men. After they landed in what is now Mexico, the explorers met with some tribes who were friendly. They also fought with others who were not. Cortés led his expedition inland, looking for the rich and powerful people who lived there. They were called Aztecs.

The first meeting between Cortés and the Aztec emperor, Montezuma, was friendly.

THE AZTEC EMPIRE

The Aztecs ruled a large and highly developed **empire**. They had a large army, which kept control over more than five million people. It was a wealthy society where trade flourished. Aztecs were farmers, artists, and craftspeople.

Montezuma was the leader of the Aztecs. At first, he welcomed Cortés and his men, but soon the Spanish and the Aztecs began fighting. Many were killed on both sides. The Aztecs held off the invaders for two years. Finally, in 1521, Cortés defeated the Aztecs and captured the capital of Tenochtitlán. Then, he had the city demolished and succeeded in destroying the Aztec empire.

Tenochtitlán

The Aztec capital was Tenochtitlán, where 150,000 people lived. It was a city built in the middle of a lake, connected to land by long roads. Tenochtitlán had markets, public **plazas**, and gardens. The largest buildings were **temples** where the Aztecs made sacrifices to their gods.

Many Aztec craftsmen and artists worked for the emperor.

THE INCA EMPIRE

The Aztec empire had been defeated, but an even larger group of Native Americans controlled another empire in South America. The Incas had a rich and advanced society with a population of about twelve million people. Their empire stretched for about 2,000 miles (3,219 km) along the Pacific coast.

The Incas were excellent farmers and used **irrigation** to grow crops. Their cities had beautiful palaces and temples. Stone roads and bridges reached from one end of their empire to the other.

FRANCISCO PIZARRO

Francisco Pizarro was another Spanish conquistador who came to the New World seeking wealth. While living in Central America, Pizarro heard stories of rich peoples to the south. He wanted to find them and take their gold.

In 1526 Pizarro and his men sailed south along the coast and made several landings in South America. Many men were killed, but Pizarro returned with a few gold objects and stories of a rich civilization to be conquered.

*The Inca people lived in **prosperity** and peace for hundreds of years before the Spanish conquistadors arrived in their land.*

PIZARRO'S VICTORY

In 1532 Pizarro led another army into South America. He captured Atahuallpa, the ruler of the Incas. Pizarro promised to release the leader if the Incas would fill a large room with treasure. The people filled the room with gold and silver objects, but Pizarro killed Atahuallpa anyway.

Pizarro's men used the Incan road system to easily travel all over the empire. The diseases brought by the Europeans weakened the Incas and other peoples, and thousands died. The invaders finally conquered the Incas, and another great empire was destroyed.

Incan treasures

The treasures taken by the Spanish were more than just gold and silver. Skilled Incan craftspeople had turned the precious metals into beautiful works of art. There were carvings, jewelry, and fine silverware. All that beauty was lost to conquistadors like Pizarro. He ordered all the gold and silver items to be melted down and made into bars, which were easier to ship back to Spain.

A few Native American treasures survived the conquest and looting of the Spanish explorers.

FIRST AROUND THE WORLD

Ferdinand Magellan was born in Portugal, where he learned navigation, geography, mathematics, and mapmaking. In 1517 he moved to Spain. Even though he knew that the Americas were in the way, Magellan still thought he could reach the Indies by sailing west. He convinced King Charles of Spain to sponsor his expedition. The king provided five ships, and Magellan sailed on September 20, 1519.

When the expedition reached South America, Magellan sailed his ships south along the coast until he found a passage to the other side. He and his men sailed through rough water to an ocean so calm that Magellan named it Pacific. This word means "peaceful."

The expedition continued west and reached the Philippine Islands, in Asia. Here, Magellan was killed while fighting with Philippine people. His men sailed on, and in September 1522, one ship with eighteen survivors made it back to Spain. Magellan's expedition became the first to sail around the world.

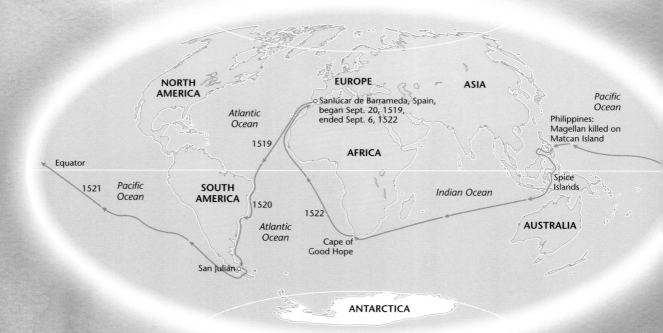

This map shows the passage that Magellan found.
It was later called the Straits of Magellan.

RAPID CHANGES

After Columbus's discovery in 1492, things changed quickly in the Americas. Settlers came to the Caribbean islands and started large farms called plantations. Explorers journeyed farther west and found new lands and people to conquer.

Conquistadors conquered the largest empires in South America and took their treasures. After Cortés destroyed Tenochtitlán, he had a new city built there and named it Mexico City. It became the capital of the colony of New Spain.

Plantation owners used slaves to work the fields.

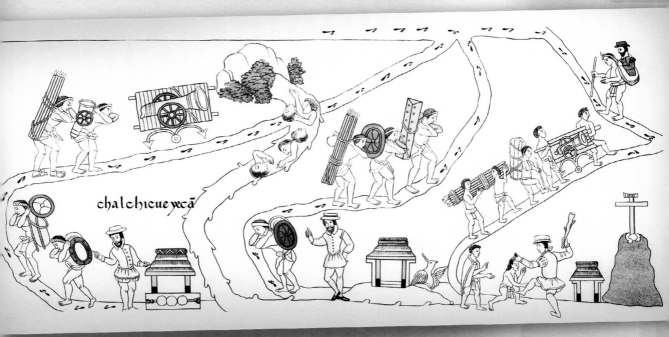

chalchicueyca

First slaves in the Americas

At first, when the Spanish settlers started plantations on Caribbean islands, they forced the Native Americans to work as slaves. In 1491 there were many thousands of Native Americans living on Hispaniola. By 1500 more than half had died from disease and abuse. This led to a shortage of slaves. By 1510 slaves were being brought in from Africa. Many more would follow. By 1520 there were no Native Americans left on the island.

EXPLORING NORTH AMERICA

The first Spanish explorer to reach the land that is now the United States was Juan Ponce de Leon. While living in Puerto Rico, he heard stories of a "fountain of youth" with water that made old people young again. In 1513 he sailed north to search for this incredible fountain.

After a month, de Leon landed on a shore with wildflowers and sweet-smelling trees. He named it Florida (meaning "flowery"), planted a cross, and claimed it for Spain. No fountain was found, but Spain now had a **claim** in North America.

A CLAIM FOR FRANCE

In 1534 Jacques Cartier made the first claim in North America for France. The king of France sent him to look for a northwest passage through the continent. Cartier landed on an island on the North American coast. He claimed it for the king, who named it Newfoundland.

Cartier made another trip in 1535. He sailed up the St. Lawrence River until he was stopped by dangerous waters.

THE SEARCH FOR GOLD

Hernando de Soto formed a large expedition to search for treasure in North America. In 1539 he sailed from Spain to the west coast of Florida with 600 men, 24 priests, and 220 horses. They marched north through what is now Georgia, South Carolina, and North Carolina and across the mountains into Tennessee.

De Soto and his men encountered Native Americans along the way and treated them cruelly, killing thousands. They reached the Mississippi River in 1541 and claimed all the lands they had explored for Spain. De Soto did not find any gold. He was still looking in 1542 when he died of fever.

Early exploring expeditions included many men and supplies.

A dangerous exploration

Álvar Núñez Cabeza de Vaca was a lucky man. He was one of only four survivors from a 400-person expedition that landed in Florida in 1528, searching for gold. Hostile Native Americans and other hardships wiped out the rest of the men. It took eight years for the four survivors to walk to Mexico City.

CORONADO'S EXPEDITION

At the same time that de Soto was exploring the southeast part of North America, an even larger Spanish expedition was marching into the southwest part. Francisco Vásquez de Coronado was the leader of this force. It included 300 soldiers and 1,000 Native American warriors. They also brought along servants, slaves, and herds of cattle and sheep for food.

Like many other Spanish explorers, Coronado was searching for cities of gold. His expedition left Mexico in 1540 and entered North America in present-day Arizona. Before long, Native Americans attacked, killing a Spanish soldier. Several of the attackers were captured, and Coronado had them hanged from trees. It was the first of many fights with the Native Americans.

The explorers traveled through lands that are now parts of New Mexico, Texas, Oklahoma, and Kansas. The trails were rough and dangerous. They traveled over mountains, deserts, and rivers.

Spanish soldiers wore heavy armor to protect them during battle.

CITIES OF MUD

Coronado found villages, but they were poor. Their houses were made of mud and straw, not gold. The Spanish invaders killed many Native Americans who attacked them and many who did not. When winter came, the soldiers forced one group of Native Americans out of their village and took their food and blankets.

Harsh conditions, Native American attacks, and diseases finally wore the expedition down. Coronado and a few survivors limped back to Mexico City. He had explored a huge area of **territory** and claimed it for Spain, but he had not found any "cities of gold."

You can still see the remains of Pueblo cliff dwellings today.

Cliff dwellers
The Native Americans whom Coronado encountered were Puebloans. The ancestors of the Pueblo people were cliff dwellers. Their houses were made of stone and clay and built high in the sides of cliffs. They were farmers and hunters. More than 200 years before Coronado arrived, a severe drought caused the ancestral Pueblo people to leave their cliff homes and move closer to rivers.

MISSIONARIES

Beside finding riches, many explorers wanted to convert Native Americans to Christianity. Their expeditions often included missionaries. Their job was to teach Native Americans about religion. Sometimes, when explorers returned home, missionaries stayed behind.

Some missionaries traveled to new territory alone to establish missions and schools. Many **missions** were located near Native American villages. Other times, Native Americans moved and settled near the missions. The missionaries taught the Native Americans about Christianity. The Native Americans taught the missionaries how to live in a new land.

Most missionaries were fair and good, but some treated Native Americans cruelly and forced them to work on mission farms and ranches. Many tribes were opposed to any new people moving into their territory. These tribes attacked missions and settlements whenever they could. Sometimes, a friendly tribe would join with missionaries and soldiers to fight against an attacking tribe.

Missionaries brought a new religion to Native Americans.

SIR FRANCIS DRAKE

Francis Drake was a daring and courageous English sea captain. Born around 1540, he spent his whole life mastering the sea, and especially fighting on the sea. He became a raider who attacked Spanish ships and ports to steal their treasure. Queen Elizabeth of England secretly approved of his activities because he shared his captured loot with her.

During a raid on Spanish settlements in Panama, Drake saw the Pacific Ocean. He decided to be the first Englishman to cross it. In 1577 he set sail from Plymouth, England. Drake guided his ship around South America, through the Straits of Magellan, and into the Pacific Ocean. He sailed north to California and claimed it for England. Then, he sailed west around the world and back to where he began.

The Golden Hind *was a grand sailing ship.*

Golden Hind
When Francis Drake left on his journey around the world, he had five ships. Only one made it all the way. It was named the *Golden Hind*. Hundreds of years later, a replica, or copy, of this ship was built, and it still sails today.

HENRY HUDSON

Henry Hudson had tried to find a northeast passage to Asia by sailing east around the top of Europe. He made two voyages funded by English merchants, but both times he had to turn back because of cold and ice.

Hudson's third expedition was sponsored by the Dutch East India Company in 1609. This time, he was looking for a northwest passage. Hudson sailed to North America, down a large river, and landed in present-day New York. Although he sailed far along the river, he did not find a passage to the Pacific Ocean. The river was later named after him, and this voyage gave the Dutch a claim on the Hudson River Valley.

Canada's Hudson Bay was named for Henry Hudson.

Hudson's last voyage
On Hudson's fourth voyage, he sailed farther north and into a large bay. He made his crew spend a long, cold winter there, trapped in the ice. By springtime they were so angry that they put Hudson, his son, and seven others in a small boat with no food and left them. The boat was never seen again.

NEW FRANCE

Many French traders were more interested in furs than gold. They started to trade with the Huron tribe that lived in the forests of North America. The French started a colony and called it New France. In 1673 the governor of the colony, still looking for a northwest passage, sent an expedition to explore a great river to the west.

Louis Joliet, a fur trader and mapmaker who had been born in New France, led the group. He was joined by Jacques Marquette, a Catholic missionary who could speak Native American languages. They set out across Lake Michigan in two canoes with five other Frenchmen and two Native American guides.

The explorers paddled up the Fox River, then the Wisconsin River, and finally reached the Mississippi River in what is now Wisconsin. They traveled along the Mississippi for some time, but finally realized it could not be the northwest passage because it flowed south.

Before paved roads, rivers were the easiest way to travel.

LA SALLE

Joliet was the first European to travel on the Mississippi, but he did not find the mouth of the river. Another Frenchman did. He was René-Robert Cavelier, known as Sieur de La Salle, or "Sir" La Salle.

La Salle had been exploring the territory around the Great Lakes. Seneca tribes taught him how to survive in the wilderness on wild animals and dried corn. He learned to use birch-bark canoes, which were light and easy to carry.

In 1682 La Salle and about 50 men paddled down the Mississippi River in canoes. They traveled south for two months and reached the mouth of the Mississippi River, where it enters the Gulf of Mexico. La Salle claimed the river and all the lands that touch it for France.

La Salle was the first European to travel down the Mississippi River to its mouth.

WOODLAND INDIANS

Many of the Native Americans encountered by all the explorers in eastern North America were known as Woodland Indians. This was because they lived in the great forests that covered the land. The Algonquian and the Iroquois were two of the main groups of Woodland Indians. Tribes like the Blackfoot and the Cree spoke the Algonquian language. The Iroquois people included the Seneca and Oneida tribes.

Woodland Indians hunted animals for food and clothing. They gathered nuts, berries, and wild fruit. Those who lived in areas with a mild climate and good soil grew corn, beans, squash, and pumpkins.

Mound Builders

The Mound Builders were the ancestors of some of the Woodland Indians. They made thousands of mounds by carrying dirt in baskets and piling it up. Many of the mounds are extremely large and some have animal shapes. At one time, the Mound Builders had a very large population and large cities. Their civilization had faded by the time the Europeans arrived, when only a few Mound Builders were left.

The Mound Builders made mounds in the shapes of animals. This one, found in Ohio, was formed like a serpent.

WORLDS COLLIDE

When explorers from Europe made contact with Native Americans, they often came into conflict. In most cases, Europeans had the advantage. The Native Americans had few defenses against these invaders from another world. The Europeans had better weapons and could kill Native Americans by the thousands.

DIFFERENT APPROACHES

Relations between Native Americans and Europeans often depended on what the Europeans wanted. For example, many of the Spanish explorers had orders to bring back gold and silver. It took a lot of effort to mine and process these metals, so the Spanish often used force to make the Native Americans work as slaves.

In some cases, the Native Americans had the upper hand in the relationship. For example, many French explorers depended on Native Americans to trap animals and bring furs to trading posts. The Native Americans received European goods in return. In some cases, they were able to set the prices for their furs.

Explorers and Native Americans sometimes had friendly meetings.

A LUCKY CONQUISTADOR

Sometimes coincidence played a big part in the outcome of a meeting. When Cortés invaded the Aztec empire, he only had a few hundred men against millions of Aztecs. But the Aztecs had a legend of a god who would arrive at a certain time. Cortés arrived at just the right time and he looked like the god in the legend. The Aztecs thought Cortés was the god, and so they let him come right into Tenochtitlán.

THE UPPER HAND

Native Americans did have one big advantage. They knew how to live on the land because it was their home. Native Americans knew where to find food and water. They could make clothing and shelter from natural materials. Many explorers died because they did not have this knowledge.

Native American languages

The Native American tribes spoke at least 250 different languages. This was a disadvantage because new ideas were hard to share. It was difficult for peoples to work together when they could not talk to each other.

Native Americans were the first people in the world to grow corn.

DEADLY DISEASES

Many Native Americans died after contact with explorers, but not from fighting. Most died from diseases. Just as they had no defenses against European weapons, their bodies had no **immunity** against new germs. Sicknesses like smallpox, measles, and mumps were deadly to people who had never been exposed to them. Among some peoples, disease killed more than 90 percent of their population.

Plenty of explorers died from sickness, too. Whenever people traveled to new places, they were exposed to new diseases. But people from Europe had protections from more diseases because they had not been set completely apart from other people. Centuries of contact with people from other countries and continents had helped them build up their immunities.

NATIVE AMERICANS TODAY

Although fighting and diseases killed much of the Native American population, some survived. Today, **descendants** of these Native Americans keep the history and customs of their ancestors alive.

Native American culture is still alive and well in the Americas.

OLD WORLD GAINS

The Old World gained the most when the two worlds collided. They explored and controlled two new, large continents that were full of **natural resources**. The treasures and products carried back to Europe made some countries richer and more powerful than ever before. Ideas and inventions that came from the Native Americans include canoes, sleeping in hammocks, and smoking tobacco.

Native American farmers

Native Americans were skilled farmers. They developed irrigation systems and learned how to use fertilizer to enrich the soil. Native Americans were the first people to grow corn, potatoes, squash, peppers, and tomatoes.

NATIVE AMERICAN LOSSES

The Native Americans suffered greatly from the meeting, but their way of life was not destroyed. For hundreds of years, many of them fought back against European explorers and settlers. They also maintained their religion and culture.

Many people gathered to see the interesting people and objects that explorers brought back from the New World.

FIRST COLONIES

The age of exploration was a time of great change in the world. By 1500 part of a New World had just been discovered. All that was known about the Americas was just that little edge where Columbus first landed. Nobody knew the size or shape of the new continents, or what they contained.

In 100 years, Europeans explored much of this New World. The size and shape were learned and added to the maps. Settlements were started and new natural resources were discovered and used. European countries established colonies to control their new lands and wealth.

By the 1600s, England, France, Portugal, Spain, and Holland all had claims in the Americas. Some parts of the New World were claimed by more than one country. European countries would fight over their claims for the next 200 years.

This map of North America in 1600 shows the territories claimed by Spain, France, and England.

The world that seemed so vast and unknown to the early explorers looks small to today's explorers from space.

A CRUEL TIME

It would be difficult to pick the worst cruelty of this period of history. Some peoples and their cultures were completely wiped out. Innocent people were taken and made to be slaves. Priceless documents were burned in the name of religion. "Civilized" nations took over faraway lands, changed their names, and ruled their people. By modern standards, this was all horrible.

In the 1500s, this was business as usual. Ideas about right and wrong were different from what they are today. People lived in a world ruled by force. The combination of religion and weapons sometimes led to violence. Leaders believed they were bringing a superior culture to a backward people and that killing the resistors was the right thing to do.

The Old World discovered the New, conquered it, and divided it. Neither world would ever be the same.

European settlements in the Americas

Date	Settlement	European Country
1521	Mexico City	Spain
1565	St. Augustine	Spain
1585	Fort Raleigh (Roanoke)	England
1607	Jamestown	England
1608	Quebec	France
1610	Santa Fe	Spain
1620	Plymouth	England

MAPS

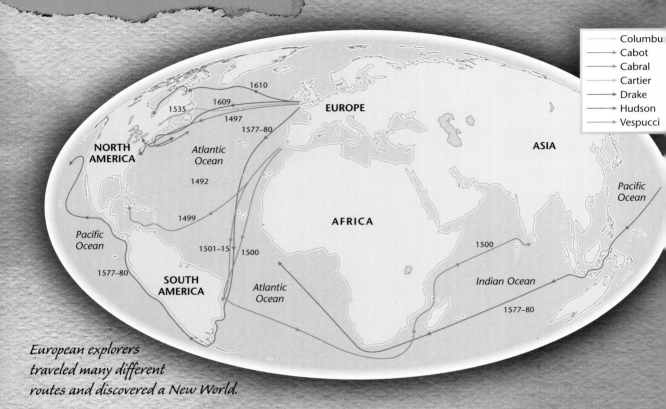

→	Columbus
→	Cabot
→	Cabral
→	Cartier
→	Drake
→	Hudson
⋯→	Vespucci

European explorers traveled many different routes and discovered a New World.

Native Americans and early explorers affected the land in the Americas. The names on this map show that their influence is still with us today.

TIMELINE

CIRCA

1000 Leif Eriksson, a Viking, lands on the east coast of North America.

1492 Christopher Columbus lands on San Salvador.

1497 John Cabot lands on the North American coast.

1500 Pedro Cabral lands in South America.

1507 The Americas are named after Amerigo Vespucci.

1508 Ponce de Leon claims Puerto Rico for Spain.

1510 Vasco Balboa founds colony at Darien in Panama.

1513 Ponce de Leon discovers Florida; Balboa sees Pacific Ocean.

1519 Hernando Cortés sails to Mexico.

1521 Cortés conquers Aztecs, claims Mexico for Spain.

1533 Francisco Pizarro conquers the Incas in Peru.

1535 Jacques Cartier sails up the St. Lawrence River.

1540 Francisco Coronado explores present-day Arizona, Kansas, New Mexico, Oklahoma, and Texas.

1541 Hernando de Soto discovers the Mississippi River.

1579 Sir Francis Drake claims the San Francisco Bay area for England.

1580 Drake completes his trip around the world.

1583 Sir Humphrey Gilbert founds the colony at Newfoundland, in present-day Canada.

1585 Colony is established at Roanoke, in present-day North Carolina.

1587 First English child is born in North America.

1609 Henry Hudson lands in present-day Maine and explores the Chesapeake Bay and Hudson River.

1610 Santa Fe is founded in what is now New Mexico.

1673 Joliet maps the Mississippi River.

1682 La Salle claims the Mississippi River and Louisiana Territory for France.

GLOSSARY

ancestor member of a family who lived a long time ago

civilization particular society or culture at a particular period in time

claim title or right to property

climate average weather conditions in a region over a long time

colonize take over and control an area

colony land not connected to a nation, yet owned and controlled by it

conquistador Spanish conqueror of the Americas in the 16th century

continent one of the seven large landmasses on Earth; Asia, Africa, North America, South America, Europe, Australia, and Antarctica

convert change people's current religion for a new one

culture ideas, customs, and manners that are shared by one group of people

descendant child, grandchild, and future generations after that

discoverer one who finds or sees something for the first time

empire large group of peoples or countries that have the same ruler, as in the Aztec empire

era particular period in history

expedition long journey for a special purpose, such as exploring

explorer one who travels to discover what a place is like

governor person elected or appointed to control a political unit

immunity having a natural protection from disease

irrigation system of ditches or pipes that supply water to crops

migrate to move from one country or region to another

mission church or other place where missionaries live or work

missionary someone who is sent by a church or religious group to teach that group's faith and do good works, quite often in a different country

natural resource material found in nature that is useful to people

passage path or route

plaza open public area, often square, that is near large buildings

prosperity success, wealth

route course that is followed from one place to another

settle to make a home or live in a new place

settlement colony or group of people who have left one place to make a home in another

slave someone who is owned by another person and thought of as property

sponsor person who is responsible for supporting another person or a group of people

temple building used for religious worship

territory area of land or region; area ruled by a government of another country

tribe group of people who share the same ancestors, customs, and laws

Viking person from one of the Scandinavian peoples who invaded and explored other countries

voyage long journey, quite often by ship

FURTHER READING

BOOKS

Blue, Rose, and Corinne J. Naden. *Exploring the Mississippi River Valley*. Chicago: Raintree, 2003.

Blue, Rose, and Corinne J. Naden. *Exploring South America*. Chicago: Raintree, 2004.

Blue, Rose, and Corinne J. Naden. *Exploring the Southwestern United States*. Chicago: Raintree, 2004.

Doak, Robin S. *Christopher Columbus: Explorer of the New World*. Minneapolis: Compass Point, 2005.

Doak, Robin S. *Hudson: Henry Hudson Searches for a Passage to Asia*. Minneapolis: Compass Point, 2003.

Englar, Mary. *Sieur de La Salle*. Mankato, Minn.: Capstone, 2005.

HISTORIC PLACES TO VISIT

The National Museum of the American Indian
4th Street & Independence Ave., SW
Washington, D.C. 20560
Visitor Information: 202-633-1000

INTERNET

Conquest of North America
http://www.vaca.com

European Explorers
http://www.cdli.ca/CITE/explorer.htm

The European Voyages of Exploration
http://www.ucalgary.ca/applied_history/tutor/eurvoya/intro.html

Primary Sources
http://www.win.tue.nl/~engels/discovery/primary.html

A Treasure Trove of North American Exploration
http://www.collectionscanada.ca/passages/

INDEX